JOHN CARLIN – ORIOL MALET

MANDELA AND THE GENERAL

Plough Publishing House

Published by Plough Publishing House
Walden, New York
Robertsbridge, England
Elsmore, Australia
www.plough.com

Originally published in French under the following title: *Mandela et le Général*

This edition is published by arrangement with Anne Edelstein Literary Agency, LLC in conjunction with its duly appointed agents L'Autre agence, Paris, France.

ISBN 978-0-87486-820-3
24 23 22 21 20 19 18 2 3 4 5

A catalog record for this book is available from the British Library.
Library of Congress Cataloging-in-Publication Data

Names: Carlin, John, 1956- author. | Malet, Oriol, illustrator.
Title: Mandela and the general / John Carlin, Oriol Malet.
Other titles: Mandela et le général. English
Description: Walden, New York : Plough Publishing House, [2018]
Identifiers: LCCN 2018024942 (print) | LCCN 2018033791 (ebook) | ISBN 9780874868357 (epub) | ISBN 9780874868364 (mobi) | ISBN 9780874868371 (pdf) | ISBN 9780874868203 (pbk.)
Subjects: LCSH: Mandela, Nelson, 1918-2013--Comic books, strips, etc. | Viljoen, Constad, 1933--Comic books, strips, etc. | Presidents--South Africa--Biography--Comic books, strips, etc. | Generals--South Africa--Biography--Comic books, strips, etc. | South Africa--Politics and government--20th century--Comic books, strips, etc. | Graphic novels.
Classification: LCC DT1974 (ebook) | LCC DT1974 .C376 2018 (print) | DDC 968.06/40922--dc23
LC record available at https://lccn.loc.gov/2018024942

Printed in the United States of America

Acclaim

"A riveting read. Carlin 'gets' Mandela. He captures powerfully Mandela's political astuteness and vast generosity. Masterful storytelling!"

Morgan Freeman

"A wonderful, accessible distillation of the genius of Mandela. In an increasingly divided political landscape, should be required reading for people of all ages everywhere."

Matt Damon

"*Mandela and the General* suspensefully reveals how Mandela's spirit of reconciliation prevailed over fear and violence in post-apartheid South Africa. Coming out as it does at a time of gathering global intolerance, this book is a timely reminder of the value of human empathy as a tool in political confrontation. John Carlin's privileged access makes this an especially exciting read."

Jon Lee Anderson, *New Yorker* staff writer, author of *Che*

"Comic books aren't just frivolous entertainment, but can be educational as well. The art by Oriol Malet has so much energy and beauty that it drew me in immediately; the scratchiness of his line work belies his skills as a master draftsman and storyteller. The story is incredibly engaging and well worth your time."

Jamal Igle, creator of *Molly Danger*, illustrator of *Black*

"Mandela is one of the greatest figures of the age, and as such we put him on a pedestal and forget the details and the challenges. Carlin simply and powerfully remind us how close South Africa came to a bloodbath and how Mandela's personal effort, persuasion, strategy, and clarity of purpose averted the ultimate tragedy to which apartheid seemed to be headed. History is not made by men or women on pedestals, but those who will bend and seek solutions rather than just stay on the high horse. This reminder is a lesson for our time as well."

Tony Marx, President and CEO, New York Public Library

"John Carlin elegantly crafts a powerful, balanced narrative well served by the evocative imagery and sequential talents of Oriol Malet. *Mandela and the General* is an important read for all who seek peace."

Andrew Aydin, co-author of *March* trilogy

"While *Mandela and the General* is told from the perspective of a man on the wrong side of history, it does not at all glorify or attempt to excuse the injustice and oppression. The banality of evil is not sugarcoated or swept under the rug, but instead is drawn clear for all to see. More importantly, at the core of this book is the notion that reason and empathy are the foundations of progress and peace."

Vita Ayala, *The Wilds* and *Livewire*

"John Carlin takes a novel approach to the true history of South Africa's struggles to end apartheid through the narrative of Constand Viljoen – general of the opposition to Nelson Mandela. It's an uncomfortable perspective through which to view an altruistic icon of change like Mandela, but the overarching theme of this graphic novel is humanization. A must-read in our current era of cultural conflict, *Mandela and the General* reminds us of what can be achieved when we view each other as human."

Kwanza Osajyefo, author of *Black*

"A concise graphic narrative of secret negotiations that helped keep the anti-apartheid struggle in South Africa from becoming even more of a bloodbath. . . . Though dialogue drives the narrative, the most striking art has the fewest words, as illustrator Malet provides historical context for the negotiations. A fascinating story with a tight focus. . . . "

Kirkus Reviews

"How Mandela talked Viljoen away from race war toward peaceful collaboration makes a fascinating parable with relevance to today's polarized politics. . . . This case study in the power of empathy to defuse conflict stands out from the often murky annals of would-be peacemaking. Will fascinate anyone interested in conflict resolution, social justice, and the history of Africa."

Library Journal, starred review

"A well-told, perceptive view of both sides in the conflict. . . . With a limited but carefully chosen color palette, Malet evokes moods as well as he depicts actions. Likenesses of Mandela and Viljoen, in particular, are realistic but never stiff or overly photographic. *Mandela and the General* is an inspirational account of historical events, including Viljoen's break with his own colleagues in pursuit of the greater good."

Foreword Reviews

To the Reader

Nelson Mandela and John Carlin on February 11, 1994

I WAS IMMENSELY FORTUNATE to be a foreign correspondent based in Johannesburg, working for the *Independent* of London, from 1989 to 1995. From the privilege of the journalist's front-row seat, I witnessed the drama of Nelson Mandela's journey from prison to the presidency, the difficult death of the racist tyranny known as apartheid, and the establishment of democracy in South Africa for the first time since the arrival of the first European settlers in 1652.

Not all the descendants of those settlers were happy to see power finally slip from their grasp, least of all a group of bitter, fearful, and heavily armed farmers who, under the leadership of a retired general called Constand Viljoen, vowed to go to war to stop black rule. Mandela's lifelong quest for freedom had pitted him against one implacable adversary after another, but none was to prove more dangerous than Viljoen, a legendary military leader in the eyes of many white South Africans.

Mandela knew that should he fail to defeat the general and the far-right cause he embodied, the dream of a democratic South Africa was in mortal peril; the nightmare, he warned, was that his country would "drown in blood."

Mandela responded as his instincts and his temperament demanded: he fought not with arms but with words; he resorted not to violence but to reason and charm. In what was to be the last great challenge in his life's mission to liberate black South Africa, he set himself the seemingly impossible task of meeting face to face with General Viljoen and persuading him not only to disarm, not only to call off the war, but to embrace the new, post-racial political order.

In putting together the story of Nelson Mandela's implausible seduction of Constand Viljoen I have drawn on numerous personal encounters with Mandela and, still more revealingly, on a conversation I had with the general himself at a beachside bar in Cape Town several years after the fateful events described in this book. I also met the general's identical twin brother, Braam Viljoen, who played a discreet but critical role in bringing about peace in South Africa.

John Carlin

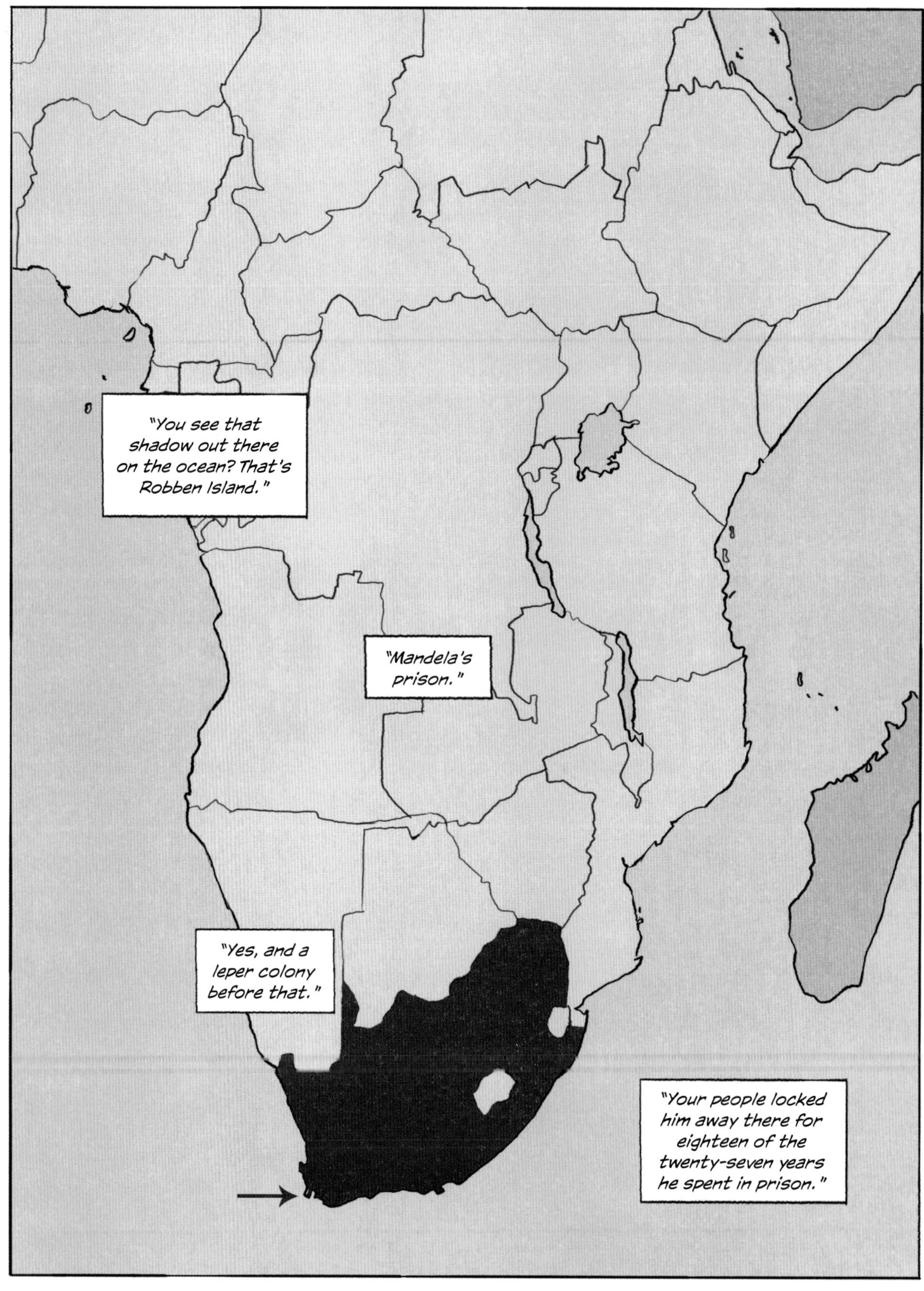
"You see that shadow out there on the ocean? That's Robben Island."
"Mandela's prison."
"Yes, and a leper colony before that."
"Your people locked him away there for eighteen of the twenty-seven years he spent in prison."

A conversation in Cape Town in a bar overlooking the Atlantic Ocean, Robben Island on the horizon.
That's very harsh, General Viljoen.
I did not regret it.

I was a soldier, he was a terrorist.
He was my number one enemy.

He fought for what he called the black liberation struggle. My duty was to defend white civilization.

Back then the role of black people was to serve us.

Sir...

"Things were so different when I was a young, up-and-coming soldier. I'll never forget one sunny winter's day in 1964 when I got leave from the army to travel to the family farm. It brings back such vivid memories."

Yes, but Constand's army promotion is not the only reason for celebration...
What do you mean?
Nelson Mandela's trial is over.

12 June 1964
Die Burger
LSON MANDELA VEROORDEEL TOT LEWE
Let me see.
He's got a life sentence.

Mmmm... I thought he would receive a death sentence.

But it's still a great day for the white nation...
...and an important victory against communism.
Let's raise a glass.
Naledi, bring the wine.

You must forgive me, but I will not drink to Mandela's imprisonment. No good will come of this.

You sound like a communist, Braam.
I am not a communist and nor, I believe, is Mandela.
He is fighting to free black people from the oppression and indignity to which we subject them.

And I fight for the freedom of the white people,
our Afrikaner *volk*,
to live in peace and prosperity.
The apartheid system is a huge injustice, Constand, and I never cease to be shocked at your failure to see it . . .
Boys, sit down and eat!

Our leader, our hope, has been jailed for life. There will be no end to apartheid now.

"Our system of racial separation had been the law since 1948. In order to uphold what we called 'civilized standards and norms' only we whites were allowed to vote."

*kaffir: an ethnic slur used to refer to a black person

That was lucky.

NON-WHITES ONLY
SLEGS NIE-BLANKES

NON WHITE
WHITE AREA

THE DIVISIONAL COUNCIL OF THE CAPE
WHITE AREA
BY ORDER SECRETARY
DIE AFDELINGSRAAD VAN DIE KAAP
BLANKE GEBIED
OP LAS SEKRETARIS

NON-WHITES ONLY
SLEGS NIE BLANKES

"It is God's wish that we should be the masters of this our beautiful land here on the southern tip of Africa."

COLORED

"And we shall continue to enjoy our earthly superiority . . ."

". . . when the time comes to join our Maker in eternal bliss. For the Scriptures tell us that we . . ."

"In order to defend our people against the threat of godless communism we were obliged to fight wars in neighboring African countries . . . . I was promoted up the ranks."

"In 1980 I was named head of the South African Defence Force by President P. W. Botha. The army, navy, and air force came under my command."

"Our theater of operations began to shift internally to combat the threat of increasingly organized black militancy."

"Increasingly violent too."

"Things are getting out of control here, General."
"We are completely outnumbered."
"I request permission to open fire."
With live ammunition?
Permission denied.
Yes, General.
But, General . . .
. . . this is a riot.
We are in danger . . .
It is not a riot, Colonel. It is a funeral.
Show some respect. Show some judgment. Show some restraint.
Understood, General. Sorry, General.
"I retired from the army in 1985 and returned to my farm."

"I ended my military career at the very top . . ."
". . . and I went into retirement powerless to stop my country descending into darkness . . ."

"...and despair. In Pretoria, our capital city ..."

"...a man called Barend Strydom opened fire against black people ..."

"...at random with a 9 mm pistol."

"By killing seven innocent bystanders he thought he had become a hero to the white nation."

"He called himself the White Wolf."

BANG!
BANG!

"That was true: he was a wild animal."

"The papers called him the smiling assassin."

"Unfortunately, some white people regarded him as a hero . . ."
BANG!

"...but in truth he was not only a savage criminal, he was a fool and a traitor to the white cause."
Because the Church Square massacre served to increase international pressure on the white government for change in South Africa?
Yes, but the pressure also increased at home, with ever greater waves of black protest.
Until finally the government eased the pressure by releasing Mandela.
I thought it was a terrible decision.

On February 11, 1990, Mandela put twenty-seven dark years of prison behind him and, at the age of seventy-one, strode out into the sunshine of a Cape Town summer's day.

MANDELA GOES FREE TODAY
For the world this is the news event of the year. For South Africa it is the news event of the century.

The destruction caused by apartheid on our subcontinent is incalculable.
There must be an end to white monopoly on political power.
We call on our white compatriots to join us in the shaping of a new South Africa.
The need to unite the people of our country is as important a task now as it always has been.
We can no longer wait.
Now is the time to intensify the struggle on all fronts.

"Mandela's release accentuated the gap between my brother and me."

Madam, we shall be off for the rest of the afternoon, if that is OK with you?
Just make sure you're back in time to serve dinner.

MANDELA RALLY AT THE STADIUM

Our day of liberation draws near!
MA
ANC
ANC
FRE
ANC

"Mandela met F. W. de Klerk, the president who ordered his release."

We must strive to find a political solution that reconciles white fears with black aspirations.

"To my great dismay, negotiations between Mandela's ANC* and the government of de Klerk started. The objective was radical political change; the venue, a conference building near Johannesburg Airport."
WORLD TRADE CENTRE
ANC
ANC

* ANC: African National Congress

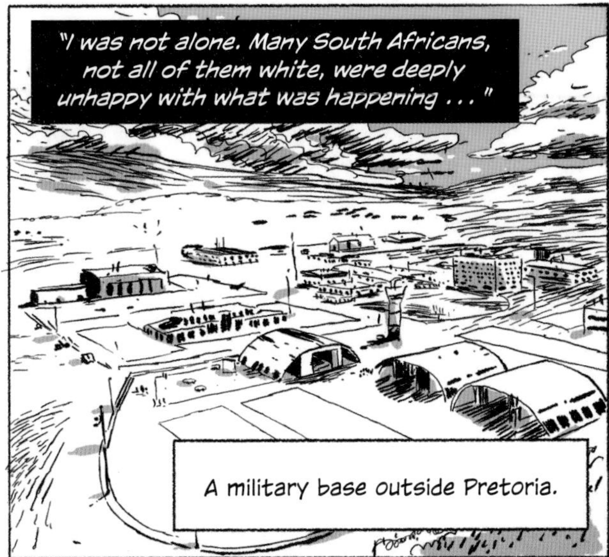
"I was not alone. Many South Africans, not all of them white, were deeply unhappy with what was happening . . ."
A military base outside Pretoria.

A Mandela government would be a disaster for all of us...

...and we must do everything–and I mean everything–in our power to stop it.

Are you with us?

Mandela sees us as traitors.

If he gets power the first thing his people will do is hang us.

4
ANC

ANC
ANC
ANC

ANC
ANC
ANC

ANC
ANC

ANC
A.N.C
POLICE
VIVA MANDELA
NOW

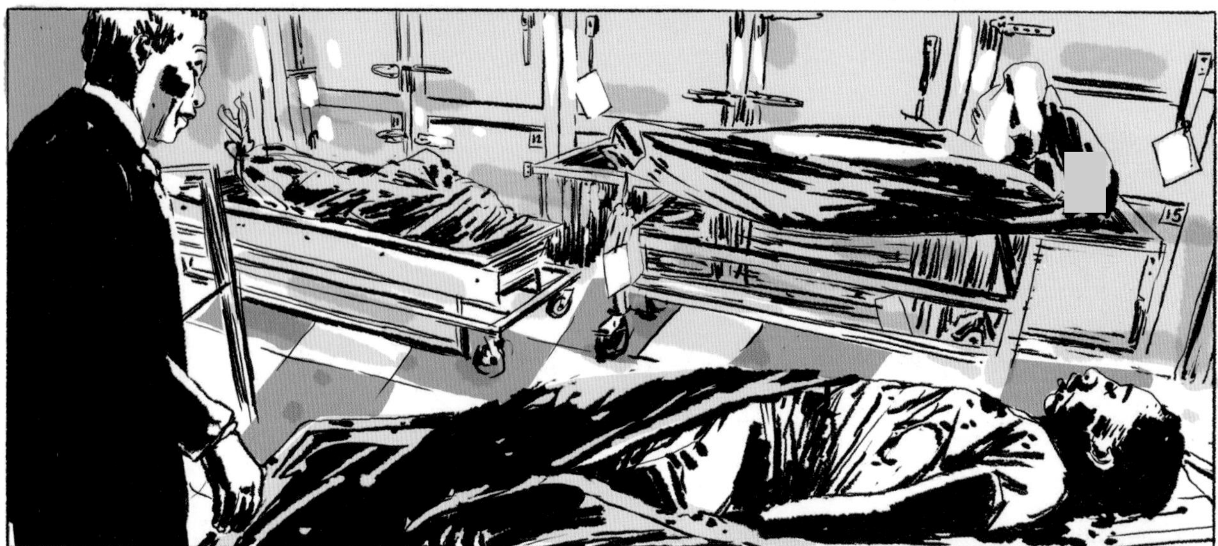

RALLY
Volsoorus Stadium - 21 Sept '92
9:30 a.m.
Mandela Speaks
ANC
X

WE WANT ARMS!
WE WANT ARMS!
WE WANT ARMS!

MANDELA, HELP US: THEY ARE KILLING US LIKE FLIES!

Do not allow yourselves to be provoked. This is what our enemies want!

They are killing us because they know we are winning and because they are afraid: democracy is in sight!

This is the nightmare that awaits us under black rule.
BLACK VIOLENCE ESCALATES

They will expel us from our lands.

The communists will close our churches.
Yes, General, and they will kill our language.

There can be only one solution: we must create our own separate white homeland to protect ourselves from Mandela and his savages.

You must help us, General! Lead us!

"Then something happened that put South Africa in peril like never before . . . Chris Hani was wildly popular among black South Africans. He was a declared communist and had been my counterpart, you might say, as the top military leader of the ANC. It had been his destiny to be Mandela's heir . . ."

Johannesburg, April 1993.

30

CHRIS!
?
BANG!
BANG!
BANG!

CAPE TIMES
with BUSINESS REPORT
11 APRIL, 1993
Chris Hani assassinated
Mandela's number two dead

Special edition
THE WEEKLY MAIL
The paper for a changing South Africa
CHRIS HANI WAS LIKE A SON TO ME
"He was a great leader, a great fighter."

11 April 1993
MORE NEWS. YOUR WAY.
The Citizen
South Africa on the edge of a precipice
"Our patience has run out!"
NEWS PAGE 4
" We will kill!"
changing South Africa
MAIL
11 April 1993
Cape Argus
AM EDITION
Race war looms
A
KILL the BOER!
KILL the FARMER!

The
South
POLICE
34
“We are leaving the country”

This is a watershed moment for all of us...

Our decisions and actions will determine whether we use our pain, our grief, and our outrage...

Didn't that address make you change your mind about Mandela, General?

No. He did calm things down, I agree, but it was he who had unleashed the tiger.

And my people were more frightened than ever.

Especially when they saw our government giving in to every demand Mandela made...

WORLD TRADE CENTRE
We have a proposal that we think will break the deadlock.
The first democratic government of South Africa will be a coalition of blacks and whites.
We hold our country's first all-race elections next year.
But it will not be "winner takes all."
CYRIL RAMAPHOSA / A N C
I believe this is a breakthrough.
I see the road ahead more clearly than ever before.
ROELF MEYER / GOVERNMENT

"Soon after, I received some visitors at the family farm. It would turn out to be a fateful day . . ."

General . . .

You are all very welcome, gentlemen.

General Viljoen, I believe you know who I am: Eugene Terre'Blanche.

I lead the Afrikaner Resistance Movement.

I represent the White Wolves!

The Resistance Against Communism!

The White Liberation Movement!

I know your organizations.

Here on my farm I follow the news closely.
What do you need from me?

We must not allow Mandela and his barbarians to steal our nation.

We must stand up, take up arms, and defeat the communist terrorists!
We are divided into too many factions, General. You are a legend in the South African military; you are the only leader capable of uniting us into one force capable of stopping Mandela.

That is God's truth!
YES!

Our backs are against the wall.
We must resist, we must fight to create our own separate homeland.
Your people need you, General.
You must lead the forces of white liberation.
This is a momentous decision you ask me to take. I do not know if this is for me. I will think about your offer.
Now, gentlemen, let us take each other's hands and pray.

"I was a military man."

"Politics was not my sphere."

"But . . ."

Potchefstroom, May 1993.
FIRM AND STEADFAST WE SHALL STAND, AT THY WILL TO LIVE OR PERISH, O SOUTH AFRICA, DEAR LAND!

We are the owners of this land!
AWB

My life belongs to my culture, my God, my language, my nation.
We stand for revolution and war!

The time has come to invite the man of the moment on stage. Allow me to say that I shall be proud, proud, very proud to serve as a soldier in the lowest rank, to be a corporal, if need be, under the leadership of our great Afrikaner hero,
General Constand Viljoen!

GENERAL!
GENERAL!
GENERAL!

A bloody confrontation is inevitable...
but we will gladly sacrifice our lives, because our cause is just.
The new Afrikaner freedom struggle has begun!
Every Afrikaner must be ready.
Every farm, every school is a target...
AWB

LEAD US, WE WILL FOLLOW!
LEAD US, WE WILL FOLLOW!
LEAD US, WE WILL FOLLOW!
LEAD US, WE WILL FOLLOW!

"One of our first shows of force was at the World Trade Centre while negotiations were underway inside between the ANC and the government . . ."
WORLD TRADE CENTRE
AWB
DEATH TO THE THE ANC
". . . but this was not the moment for violent confrontation, in my judgment, and I found myself acting rather uncomfortably as a peacemaker between my supporters and the police."
"Things could have gone a lot worse, yet I was not as successful as I might have wished . . ."
God help us!
They've broken inside . . .

GOD, BLOOD, WAR

WHITE NATION!

Where have the scum politicians gone?

They've locked themselves inside an office like scared rats.

Mr. Terre'Blanche!
Yes, General?
Mr. Terre'Blanche, order your men to withdraw.
Now.
"It was a miracle that no blood was shed."

"The Voortrekker Monument is a powerful symbol for us. It commemorates our brave Afrikaner pioneers in the 19th century."

and set up clandestine cells so that on the appointed day we may strike the decisive blow for our freedom.

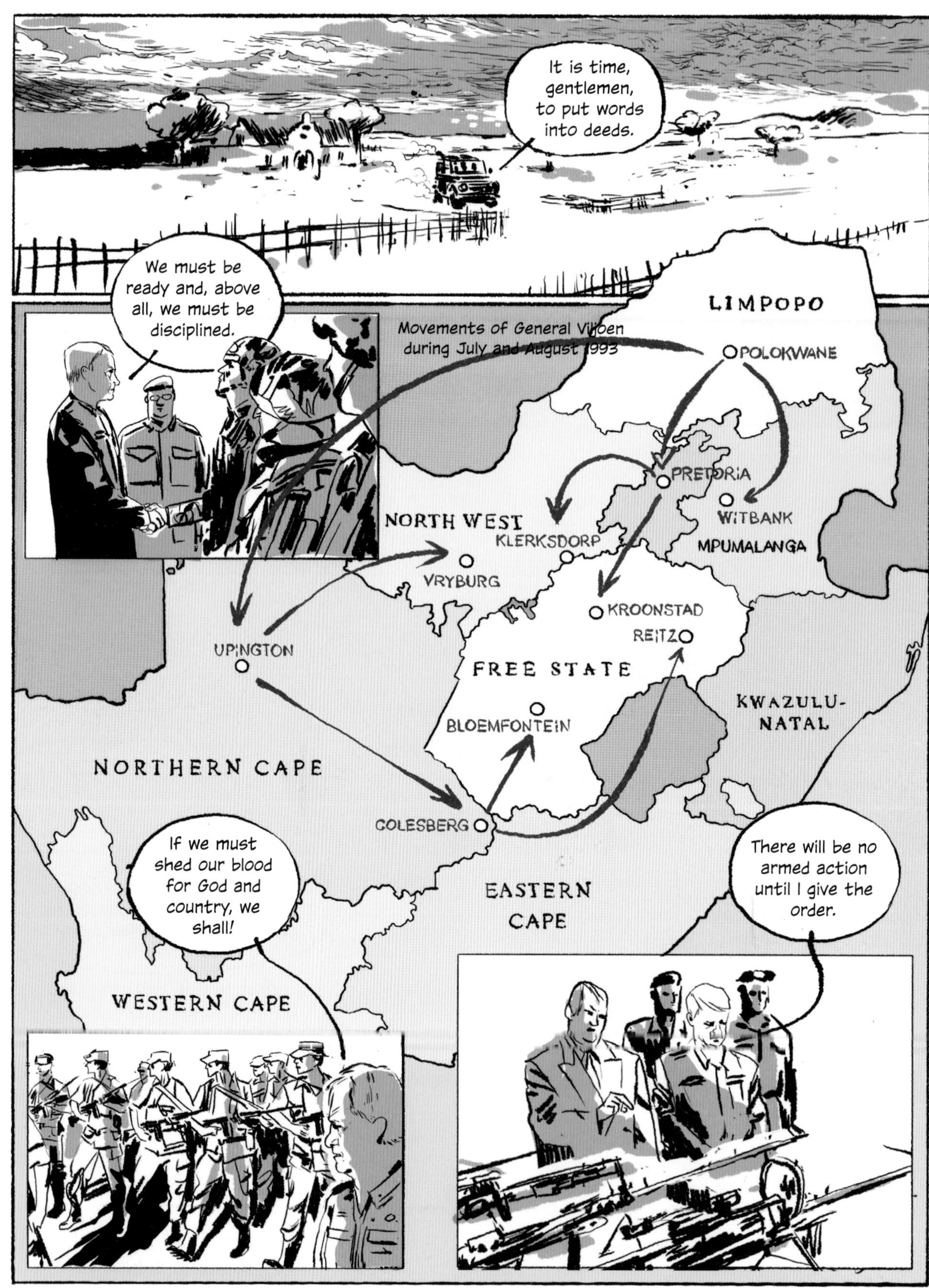
It is time, gentlemen, to put words into deeds.
We must be ready and, above all, we must be disciplined.
Movements of General Viljoen during July and August 1993
LIMPOPO
POLOKWANE
PRETORIA
WITBANK
MPUMALANGA
NORTH WEST
KLERKSDORP
VRYBURG
KROONSTAD
REITZ
UPINGTON
FREE STATE
BLOEMFONTEIN
KWAZULU-NATAL
NORTHERN CAPE
COLESBERG
EASTERN CAPE
WESTERN CAPE
If we must shed our blood for God and country, we shall!
There will be no armed action until I give the order.

"... and a large black hand came up from under the floor and grabbed me by the ankle."

Pretoria, a few days later.
General, we have a plan.

There is a congress of the ANC leadership next month. We can . . .
We can plant a bomb.

No.
Categorically no!
We are warriors, not murderers!

"These so-called Afrikaner freedom fighters are trying to hold back the clock of history."

"They are seeking to drown democracy in blood. They call us terrorists; they are the terrorists now."

Is it still "no"?

beep! beep! beep!

Braam! How are you, brother?
Constand, we must meet.

I have a message
from Mandela.

You have what?
You've seen him?
I have seen him.
He wants to meet.

With me?

With you.
In secret.
The prize
would be
peace.

And the price
of peace,
Braam?
Surrender?
Betrayal of
my people?
See him,
Constand.
What do you
have to lose?

Mandela's home, Johannesburg, October 1993.

Ah, hello, General. How very good to see you! I have heard so much about you.

Thank you very much for accepting my invitation.
It's... It's a pleasure for me too...

Did you travel far?
I believe you have a farm in the eastern Transvaal...
Yes...
...a beautiful part of the world!
General...
...would you mind if before our delegations meet you and I had a brief conversation in private?
Have a seat, please.

Do you take tea, General?
Yes, please, Mr. Mandela.

Do you take milk?
A little, please.

Some sugar?
One spoon, please.

General . . .

I understand you are planning to go to war against us.

I think I know why.

I have gotten to know your people well down the years.

I have read your people's history. As you can hear, I speak your language. I understand your fears. I can see why you would want to go to war. In your place, and had I had your upbringing, I might want to do the same.

And, General, I know too that you have the guns and the manpower to cause terrible bloodshed in this country. You are stronger militarily than us, but we have the numbers. And we will have the international support.
I put it to you, General, that if you go to war as you propose, all we will end up with will be the peace of cemeteries. Would you agree?

Mr. Mandela, in all honesty I cannot disagree with your analysis. And I have to say that I know what war is and I know what it is to speak to the widows and mothers of dead soldiers.
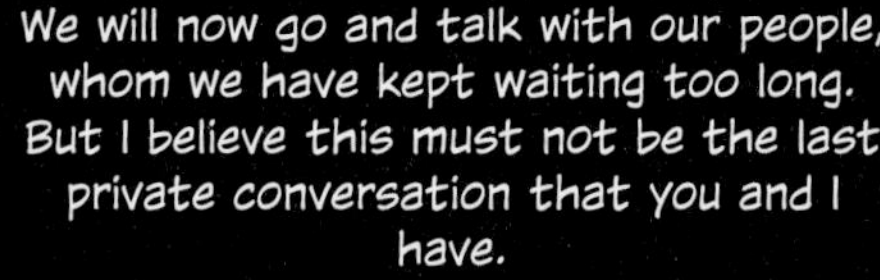
We will now go and talk with our people, whom we have kept waiting too long. But I believe this must not be the last private conversation that you and I have.

I believe we must carry on meeting, discreetly, to see if we can find a way that will reconcile your people's understandable fears with my people's legitimate aspirations.
Agreed, Mr. Mandela. We must try at least.
Let us shake hands on this, General. Peace must be our goal. Peaceful coexistence between your people and mine.

I cannot deny I was surprised.

I was impressed.

I had much food for thought.

Yet the reality was that our people lived in ever greater fear.

CAPE TIMES
with BUSINESS REPORT
ST JAMES' CHURCH MASSACRE
11 WHITES DEAD
DISSIDENT BLACK TERRORIST GROUP BLAMED

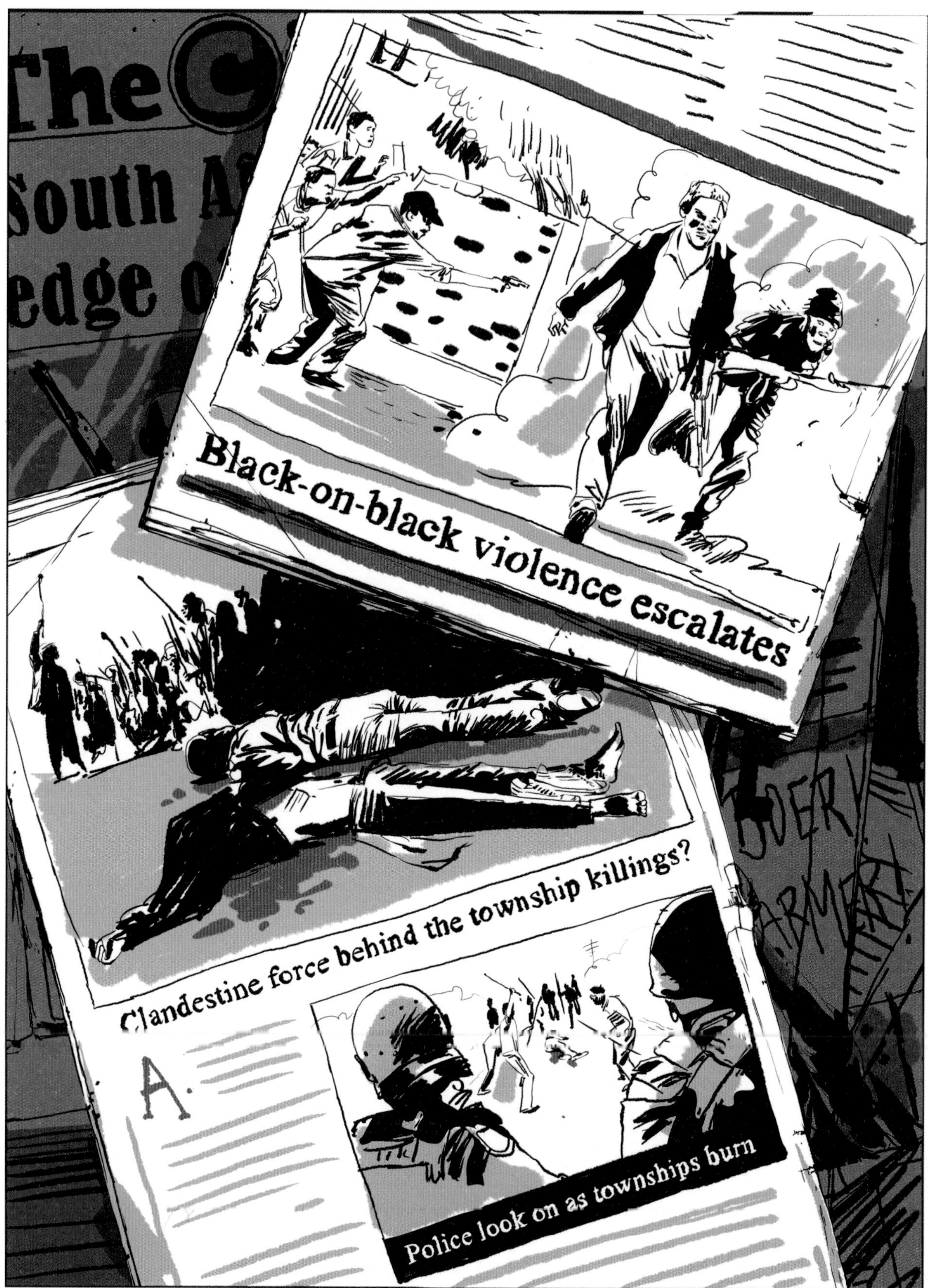
The
South
edge
Black-on-black violence escalates
Clandestine force behind the township killings?
A.
Police look on as townships burn

Johannesburg, Shell House, the ANC headquarters, November 1993.
1 PLEIN ST.
Big mistake to meet with that fascist Viljoen!

We want peace. But must we beg on our knees for it?
Where is our dignity?

True! Are we cowards?

Are we not strong enough to defeat this white trash?

Must we always turn the other cheek?

I will not tolerate this language to describe General Viljoen!
He is misguided politically due to circumstances of his birth, of his time, and of his place. But he is a man of honor.
That may be true...
...but the armed organization he leads represents the greatest threat to everything we have fought for all our lives.
Yes, Viljoen has his finger on the trigger.
He can murder democracy and means to do so.

Yes...
...and he is also the only man who can stop this war on democracy.
We must put ourselves in his shoes if we are to defeat him.
How do you think you would have thought about us, the ANC, if you had been brought up white and deeply religious on a remote farm and then fought in the army, indoctrinated to believe that we are godless communists?
The first lesson of war is know your enemy.
Be mature, be rational!
ANC
Only by persuasion can we achieve lasting peace in this country, only then can we achieve justice.
Or do you want endless war, just like the general's more ruthless followers do?

Look at these headlines: "Elections in April"
"ANC and Government Agree New Constitution"

It is time to act!
DIE BURGER
VERKIESINGS IN AP
"ANC EN
STEM SAAM
MET NUWE
GRONDWET"
Yes, our men are armed and ready to respond to your orders, General.

Gentlemen, I hear you. But I have called this meeting to discuss another matter. What I'll tell you must not leave this room. I ask all of you to swear in the name of God that it will remain secret.
What's happening, General?

DIE
I have met with Mandela.

You did what, General?

Seriously?

What kind of a man was he?

He spoke our language very well. He was respectful, courteous, and apparently honest.

General, you can't be serious!

And what he said, I have to recognize, made some sense.

A black man? Intelligent? Rational?

More rational than some people I know...

Mandela is an animal! He is a terrorist! A criminal! He hates our people!

He may hate our people, but put yourself in his shoes...

December, 1993.
"Merry Christmas, General!"
"Merry Christmas, Mr. Mandela!"

A cookie, General?
Thank you. Won't you have one?
No, no, I must watch my diet.

Is this why you look so fit and healthy?
No, General, it's because I spent twenty-seven years loafing on an island.

I put it to you that you should call off your armed struggle, General, take part in the elections-with a new party, if need be-and fight for your people's interests within a democratic system. Believe me when I say, General, that under my presidency there shall be no revenge against white people, there shall be no discrimination, and I shall give equal weight to the concerns of your people and mine.
And the white homeland we seek, Mr. Mandela?
I see no movement there from you.
We shall discuss your proposals for a white homeland. I shall govern for all South Africans irrespective of their race, religion, or color.

No politics today.
No politics, agreed.

Naledi . . .
Yes, Master Braam?

What is your opinion of Nelson Mandela?

Well, Master, I . . . I . . . don't know . . .

Speak freely, Naledi. My brother would appreciate that.

Well...
Master Constand...
Master Braam...
I believe Mandela is a kind man, an honest man, a great man.

What did you think, General?

My people's fate hung on my decision. I had to ask myself two questions.
Could I trust Mandela?

The answer increasingly was yes.

But did he carry his people with him?

I tended to believe that yes, he did.

Then early in 1994 my brother told me about a meeting Mandela chaired of the National Executive of the ANC.
He told his "comrades" they should prepare for power, that they had to make some important decisions, starting with what our new national anthem would be.

Well, first of all, the old white anthem must go.
Yes, that racist celebration of the white conquest of Africa: no more.
To the scrap heap of history!
And our ancient song of protest, "Nkosi Sikelel' iAfrika," this must be the new national anthem!

YES!!!

I thought you were mature leaders.
I thought you were pragmatic. I thought you had in mind the future stability of our new democracy. I see that I was mistaken.
No, I urge you all to vote to keep the old anthem and to forge a new one that will incorporate "Nkosi Sikelel' iAfrika."
We will sing both, one after the other. This will be our new national anthem.
"Mandela's motion was approved unanimously by the ANC's National Executive."

January 29, 1994.
Pretoria.
Nothing can stop the Afrikaner from obtaining his freedom!
Never!
Nothing!
Nothing will stop us!
However, while we are armed and ready to die if need be, violence must only be a last resort.

If possible, we should aim to achieve our goals by peaceful means.
NO!
NO!

We should open our minds and contemplate the possibility, just the possibility, of pressing for an Afrikaner homeland politically, not by force of arms.

TRAITOR!
JUDAS!

WHAT A DISGRACE!
BLACK-LOVER!
SELL-OUT!

WE WANT WAR!
NOW!
WE WANT WAR!
NOW!

Well done, brother.

Well done! What have I done?
My people are divided. I am losing my credibility with them.
This is the test of a leader, Constand. If your people are mistaken, you must tell them.
Maybe it is me who is mistaken.

They call you a traitor, but a traitor can also be a man who has the courage to go against the current and stand up for what he believes.
That is what you are. You have adapted to the new reality.

You have been true to all South Africans,
not just to your own.

I have always known you are a good man, Constand.
You will do the right thing.

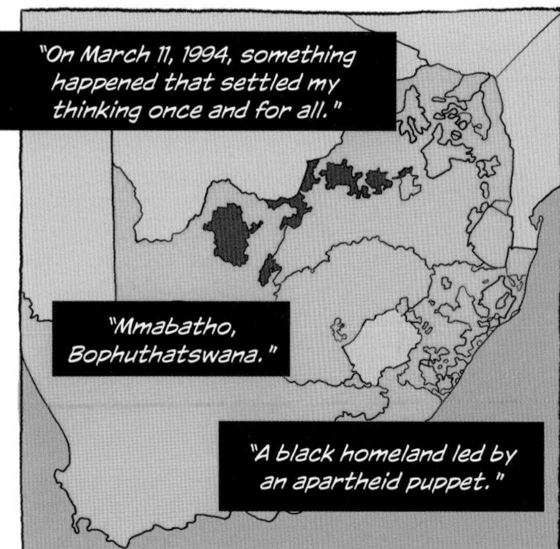
"On March 11, 1994, something happened that settled my thinking once and for all."
"Mmabatho, Bophuthatswana."
"A black homeland led by an apartheid puppet."

"A vast ANC crowd is demonstrating."
ANC

"A large force of heavily armed AWB* men led by Terre'Blanche enters the town in a convoy of vehicles . . ."

". . . to fight the ANC."

"Many are drunk, among them Terre'Blanche."

"They fire a few shots at the black protesters, but miss."
BANG!
BANG!
BANG!

*AWB: Afrikaner Weerstandsbeweging, or Afrikaner Resistance Movement

"Three uniformed AWB men crash their car and find themselves isolated and alone."
"A black policeman shoots them dead on the street."
"An image of the demise of the far right and the rise of black power."
"The South African Army enters the town and orders the AWB men out."
"They leave in chaos and shame."

The shameful episode recently involving the AWB has settled my thinking once and for all.

Sheer bloody murder

I have prayed to God for guidance...

...and I have concluded that war would be futile. We have the guns but we are outnumbered. The whole world will be against us.

We would kill and be killed for nothing.

We would die with honor, General!

"That moment marked the birth, the painful birth, of the Afrikaner Freedom Front, our new political party."

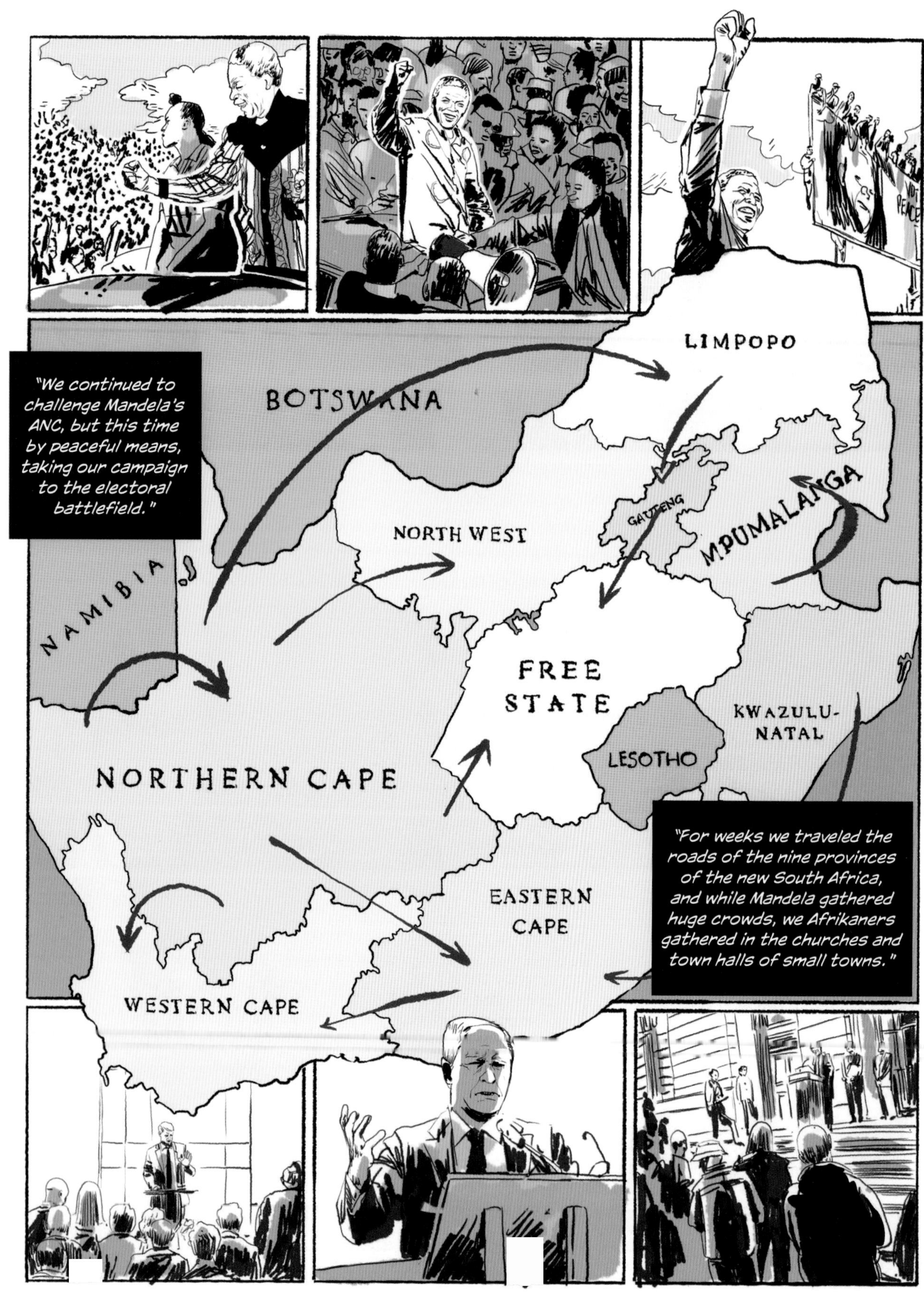

"We continued to challenge Mandela's ANC, but this time by peaceful means, taking our campaign to the electoral battlefield."
LIMPOPO
BOTSWANA
GAUTENG
MPUMALANGA
NORTH WEST
NAMIBIA
FREE STATE
KWAZULU-NATAL
LESOTHO
NORTHERN CAPE
EASTERN CAPE
WESTERN CAPE
"For weeks we traveled the roads of the nine provinces of the new South Africa, and while Mandela gathered huge crowds, we Afrikaners gathered in the churches and town halls of small towns."

VRYHEIDSFRONT
Steun
Genl Constand Viljoen
VRYHEIDSFRONT
Steun
Genl Constand Viljoen
VRYHEIDSFRONT
VRRRUM!

Let us hope the General's party wins a few seats in Parliament.

It would not be a good thing if they were to be humiliated.

THE WEEKLY MAIL
The paper for a changing South Africa
25 Apr. 1994.
Terrorist bomb at a crowded bus stop kills a dozen black civilians
Mandela: "We shall not be intimidated."

"Mandela was right. The electoral train had left the station and there was no stopping it now."
CAPE TIMES
with BUSINESS REPORT
Thursday, April 28, 1994
Vote, the beloved country!
Now is the time!
The dream has come true!
Desmond Tutu: "It's like falling in love!"

MORE NEWS. YOUR WAY.
The Citizen
An overwhelming victory for Mandela's ANC.
NEWS PAGE 4
NEWS PAGE 4
changing South Africa
MAIL
5 MAY 1994
Cape Argus
AM EDITION
Viljoen's party gets 9 seats in the newdemocratic national assembly parliament to the ANC's 252
VF

Cape Town, May 12, 1994.
The opening of the new Parliament.

General, it is very good to see you here!

I thank you, General.
I thank you.

"He was my president. I was a military man. I responded as a military man must."

How long did you remain in Parliament, General?
Five years, the same as Mandela.
He had set an example to Africa and the world by voluntarily relinquishing the presidency after just one term in power.

I gave a speech in Parliament to mark the occasion.
"Go and have yourself a well-earned rest, Mr. President."
"Go and lie in the shadow of a tall tree."

Thanks to Mandela so many lives were saved. So much suffering was avoided.

Mandela is the greatest of men.

Goodbye.
Goodbye, and thank you, General.

Johannesburg, 2009. Mandela's home.
"Mr. Mandela?"
"Ah, hello, John. How are you?"
"Fine, thank you. And you?"
Mr. Mandela?
Mandela...
...can you hear me?
Mr. Mandela, does the name Viljoen strike a chord?
Constand Viljoen?
Ah, yes, the military man...
...the general.

My people said I was afraid. They said I was a coward because I reached out to the general, to the Afrikaners. But I did not engage my people in the debate. I said nothing to them. I knew I was right. I knew this was the only way to peace. And after some time they understood I was right. They have seen the results.
We have peace.

Nelson Mandela died peacefully, age ninety-five, on December 5, 2013. Constand Viljoen continues to live and work on his farm.

From the Archives

THE GENERAL THREATENS WAR

IN NOVEMBER 1993, John Carlin, South Africa bureau chief for the *Independent*, a British newspaper, files this story drawing attention to alarmingly belligerent statements in a speech by Constand Viljoen, leader of the Volksfront.

[. . .] Yesterday, General Viljoen, former South African Defense Force chief who heads the separatist Afrikaner Volksfront, tried to explain what the right want and what they will do if they do not get it. "Things are bad," he said, because of a lack of investor confidence; because of intimidation especially "among our black people"; because of "undue pressure" on South Africa from the outside world to find a quick political solution; because the government had fallen prey to "naïve idealism"; because the ANC believed, no less naïvely, that "instant nationship" was possible.

"You can't build a nation like a cup of instant coffee, just mixing in the coffee, the white milk, the brown sugar and the colorless water."

"Things can get worse" if the government and ANC "pressed on regardless." And this, it seemed, was what they intended to do. "No real decision has been taken by the government to accommodate the Freedom Alliance." In other words, self-determination, the creation of a separate state for Afrikaners, was not on the government agenda. Accordingly, "the right wing might resort to more mass action and more armed action."

Most of the questions to the general sought clarification of "armed action." Would the armed forces rise up with the right? "If any government tries to force an unacceptable solution on the Afrikaners it would happen naturally."

Ten days ago the Volksfront urged its supporters to mobilize, polish their weapons, and store rations. What did this mean? "We are not saying people must prepare for war. We say to our people, prepare to defend yourselves." Against whom? "Against terrorist groups… You must bear in mind the anger among the Afrikaner people – it could get out of control."

From the Independent, *November 10, 1993*

John Carlin in Pretoria hears a stark warning from a leading spokesman of th

Viljoen up fear

General Constand Viljoen taking the salute at a ceremony in 1985 to mark the withdrawal of South African troops from Angola Photograph: Greg English/Link

THE INDEPENDENT

SUMMARY

Mandela free but defiant

The struggle must go on, ANC leader tells joyful crowd

At least 16 are killed in clashes

INSIDE

ST VALENTINE'S DAY MISCHIEF

The *Independent,* November 10, 1993, *top* and February 12, 1990, *bottom*

THE PRISONER BECOMES PRESIDENT

IN JUNE 1994, a few weeks after the elections, President Nelson Mandela tells John Carlin of his ongoing determination to chart a middle way between black aspirations and white fears.

We are ten minutes into the interview when a white woman, a junior member of staff, walks into the wood-paneled presidential chamber office carrying a tray with two cups of tea and a glass of mineral water.

Nelson Mandela, debonair in an immaculately tailored dark suit, springs to his feet, ram-rod straight. "Good morning," he smiles. "How are you?"

"Fine, Mr. Mandela." He introduces the woman, who says her name is Lenoy Coetzee. "The water's for you, Mr. Mandela."

"Thank you very much."

It was not the occasion to engage in further conversation with Ms. Coetzee but the chances are that she has been working at the Union Buildings, the seat of government in Pretoria, for some time. Certainly since before Mr. Mandela's inauguration as president on 10 May. [...]

Was he surprised at the degree to which whites appeared to have adapted to the political changes?

He was excited by the question. "You know, that is perfectly true. Yes. Look at the lady who brought in the tea. Look at this: It is really unbelievable the way they have just adjusted to the new position. And you can also take the politicians, people like de Klerk, the way they have adjusted to their position in public functions. They do not push themselves."

How did he explain it?

"I think it is people, the nature of the human being. People want peace. They want security for themselves and for their children. I think also there are many men and women of all groups who want to contribute to the development of South Africa and this is their chance and they have seized it.

"No, this has really been remarkable, absolutely remarkable to see on television the Afrikaner farmers queuing with their black workers to vote and even chatting to them. It's really remarkable." He smiles and looks away, as if to savor the consummation of a lifelong dream. His voice trails off. "Remarkable. Remarkable..."

From the Independent, *June 8, 1994*

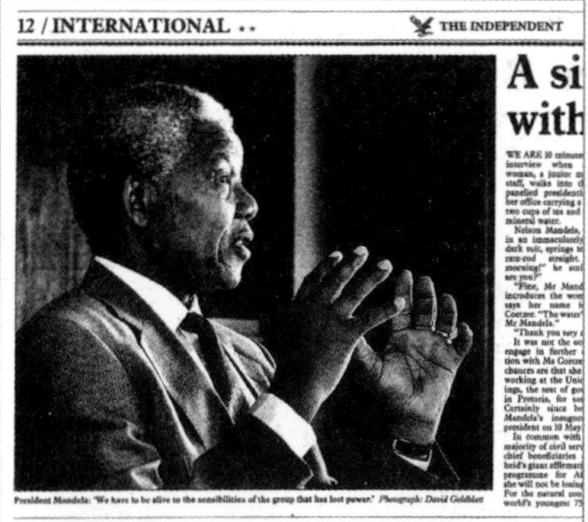

12 / INTERNATIONAL •• THE INDEPENDENT

A si
with

President Mandela: 'We have to be alive to the sensibilities of the group that has lost power.' *Photograph: David Goldblatt*

The *Independent,* June 8, 1994, *top*
Nelson Mandela and John Carlin, 1992, *bottom*

About the ANC

THE AFRICAN NATIONAL CONGRESS was founded in 1912 during a meeting that brought together religious leaders, lawyers, intellectuals, and traditional chiefs. The organization found a second wind in 1944 with the creation of a branch dedicated to the youth, the ANC Youth League. Nelson Mandela and two other leaders – Oliver Tambo and Walter Sisulu – were members and later played decisive roles. In 1948, the National Party came to power and apartheid became law. This ushered in a period of activism and resistance in the black population. In 1960, the ANC was declared illegal; as a consequence, 1961 saw the creation of the military branch of the ANC, Umkhonto we Sizwe (Spear of the Nation), led by Mandela. He was arrested in 1962, and the other leaders of the Umkhonto were arrested in 1963. In 1964, Mandela was condemned to life in prison during the famous Rivonia Trial (the sentence proved to be less harsh than expected, since the prosecution had initially demanded the death penalty).

In 1990, while the National Party was still in power, President F. W. de Klerk lifted the sanctions on the ANC, which then became legal; at the same time, he ordered the release of Nelson Mandela.

Timeline

1652

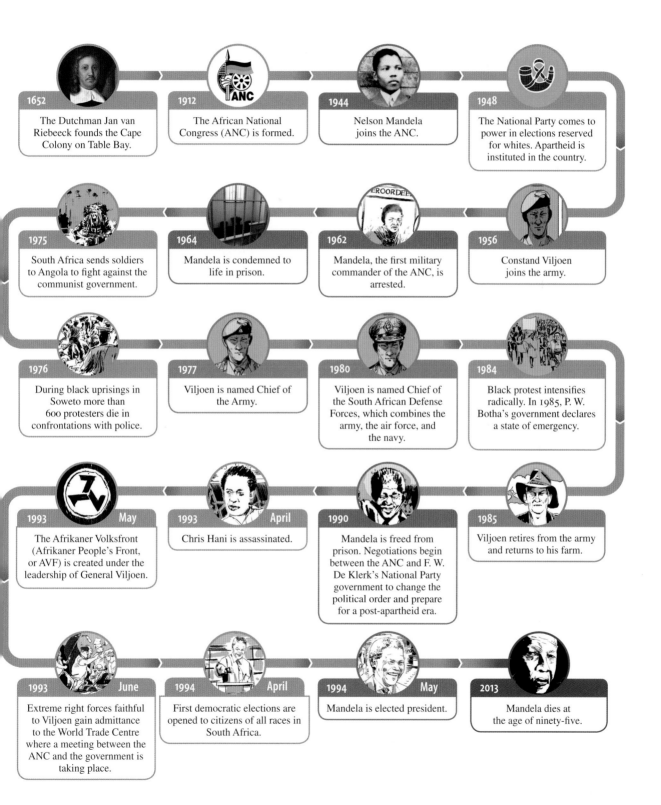

The Dutchman Jan van Riebeeck founds the Cape Colony on Table Bay.

1912

The African National Congress (ANC) is formed.

1944

Nelson Mandela joins the ANC.

1948

The National Party comes to power in elections reserved for whites. Apartheid is instituted in the country.

1956

Constand Viljoen joins the army.

1962

Mandela, the first military commander of the ANC, is arrested.

1964

Mandela is condemned to life in prison.

1975

South Africa sends soldiers to Angola to fight against the communist government.

1976

During black uprisings in Soweto more than 600 protesters die in confrontations with police.

1977

Viljoen is named Chief of the Army.

1980

Viljoen is named Chief of the South African Defense Forces, which combines the army, the air force, and the navy.

1984

Black protest intensifies radically. In 1985, P. W. Botha's government declares a state of emergency.

1985

Viljoen retires from the army and returns to his farm.

1990

Mandela is freed from prison. Negotiations begin between the ANC and F. W. De Klerk's National Party government to change the political order and prepare for a post-apartheid era.

1993 April

Chris Hani is assassinated.

1993 May

The Afrikaner Volksfront (Afrikaner People's Front, or AVF) is created under the leadership of General Viljoen.

1993 June

Extreme right forces faithful to Viljoen gain admittance to the World Trade Centre where a meeting between the ANC and the government is taking place.

1994 April

First democratic elections are opened to citizens of all races in South Africa.

1994 May

Mandela is elected president.

2013

Mandela dies at the age of ninety-five.